Breitkopf u. Härtel, Leipzig

Johannes Brahms

Complete Symphonies

in Full Score

The Vienna Gesellschaft der
Musikfreunde Edition

Edited by Hans Gál

Dover Publications, Inc., New York

Contents

	page
Editor's Preface (*Revisionsbericht*)	v
Symphony No. 1 in C Minor, Op. 68	1
Un poco sostenuto. Allegro	1
Andante sostenuto	28
Un poco Allegretto e grazioso	37
Adagio. Più andante. Allegro non troppo, ma con brio	46
Symphony No. 2 in D Major, Op. 73	87
Allegro non troppo	87
Adagio non troppo	115
Allegretto grazioso (Quasi Andantino). Presto ma non assai	125
Allegro con spirito	135
Symphony No. 3 in F Major, Op. 90	161
Allegro con brio	161
Andante	187
Poco Allegretto	198
Allegro	208
Symphony No. 4 in E Minor, Op. 98	247
Allegro non troppo	247
Andante moderato	276
Allegro giocoso	288
Allegro energico e passionato	314

Published in Canada by General Publishing Company, Ltd.,
30 Lesmill Road, Don Mills, Toronto, Ontario.
Published in the United Kingdom by Constable and Company, Ltd.

This Dover edition, first published in 1974, is an unabridged republication of
Volumes 1 and 2, entitled *Symphonien für Orchester*, of the collection *Johannes
Brahms; Sämtliche Werke; Ausgabe der Gesellschaft der Musikfreunde in Wien*,
originally published by Breitkopf & Härtel, Leipzig (n.d.; Editor's Preface to Volumes
1 and 2 dated Spring, 1926).
   The English translation of the Editor's Preface (*Revisionsbericht*) was prepared
specially for this Dover edition.

International Standard Book Number: 0-486-23053-8
Library of Congress Catalog Card Number: 74-75930

Manufactured in the United States of America
Dover Publications, Inc.
180 Varick Street
New York, N. Y. 10014

Editor's Preface

SYMPHONY NO. 1 IN C MINOR, OP. 68

Basic Texts for the Present Edition:

1. The score published by Simrock (publication number 7957). Title: "Symphonie [c moll] für grosses Orchester von Johannes Brahms. Op. 68."
2. Brahms's personal copy of the score, with entries in his own hand, in the collection of the Gesellschaft der Musikfreunde, Vienna.
3. The original manuscript of the 2nd, 3rd and 4th movements, in the collection of the N. Simrock publishing house, Berlin.

The Simrock score (published 1877) contains a few completely negligible engraving errors (missing natural signs after accidentals, missing slurs and dots in divided parts, etc.). A few corrections entered in the personal copy were already made in a later printing. Originally the coda of the 1st movement was marked *Poco sostenuto* instead of *Meno Allegro* (and still appears thus in the Eulenburg miniature score). In the last movement, the 1st half of the 6th measure after the letter E in the 2nd violin part originally read:

This version, improved in the original manuscript and in Brahms's personal copy and already corrected in the Simrock score, is still to be found in the Eulenburg score.

The oboe theme in measures 17 ff. of the 2nd movement appears without slurs in the Simrock score and even in the original manuscript. The slurs printed here were entered by Brahms in his personal copy. The oboe slur in measures 2–4 after the letter B in the same movement is also based on a correction in the personal copy (this passage lacks the slur in the Simrock score).

The original manuscript bears indications of a few later additions, among which the following are most worthy of notice:

The end of the *Andante* was originally 2 measures shorter (the 2nd and 3rd measures from the end were inserted subsequently).

The 2nd A-flat section in the 3rd movement was originally considerably shorter (the 10th measure after the letter E was followed immediately by the coda, 21st measure before the end).

In the coda of the last movement, measures 11 and 12 on page 82 were added later.

SYMPHONY NO. 2 IN D MAJOR, OP. 73

Basic Texts for the Present Edition:

1. The score published by Simrock (publication number 8028).
2. Brahms's personal copy of the score, in the collection of the Gesellschaft der Musikfreunde, Vienna.
3. The original manuscript of the score, in the collection of the N. Simrock publishing house, Berlin.

The score, published in 1878, is free of error (aside from such trivial things as missing slurs and staccato marks in divided parts and missing natural signs after accidentals, etc.). Brahms's personal copy contains no corrections, only entries which indicate that it was used for conducting.

The examination of the original manuscript yielded nothing of importance for the preparation of this edition.

SYMPHONY NO. 3 IN F MAJOR, OP. 90

Basic Texts for the Present Edition:

1. The score published by Simrock (publication number 8454).
2. Brahms's personal copy of the score, in the collection of the Gesellschaft der Musikfreunde, Vienna.
3. The original manuscript of the score, in the collection of Dr. Jerome Stonborough, Vienna.

The symphony was completed in 1883 and published in 1884. The score bears the title: "Dritte Symphonie (F dur) für grosses Orchester von Johannes Brahms. Op. 90." Below is the date 1884. The personal copy contains a fair number of emendations, which have already been made in the current Simrock score, on the occasion of some later printing. The original manuscript bears no date, only the (much later) dedication: "Seinem herzlich geliebten Hans von Bülow in treuer Freundschaft. Johannes Brahms, Wien, 8. Januar 1890." The manuscript contains a great number of later improvements entered in pencil, which were obviously made upon the first hearing of the work. The more interesting alterations are listed below. With regard to the preparation of the present edition, the examination of the manuscript showed that there was no necessity for correcting the practically faultless Simrock score.

1st movement: The change from clarinets in B-flat to clarinets in A in the 2nd subject was made at a later stage. The final chord in the trombones originally occurred in the 2 preceding measures as well.

2nd movement: In the first 4 measures after the letter E,

there was originally a drum roll on C. This drum passage, and 2 later ones (measures 6–12 after the letter G, along with the double basses, and

in the 2 final measures), were deleted afterwards, as was the only trumpet passage in the movement, in the 6th and 7th measures after E:

On the 1st page of the score of the movement the trumpet and drum systems are explicitly crossed out.

3rd movement: The C in the horns in the measure before the letter F was added subsequently.

4th movement: In measures 3–5 after the letter F, the bassoons were added later. In the measure after the letter F, the trombones were added later, and the drums apparently only while publication was in progress. The trombones and drums are also a later addition in the parallel passage, the 13th measure before the letter N. Likewise the contrabassoon in the 2 measures before N. The designation *Un poco sostenuto* in the 7th measure after O was also a later addition, which indicates that what is wanted here is really only a nuance of execution and not a completely new, much broader tempo. In the final measure there was originally a drum roll on F.

SYMPHONY NO. 4 IN E MINOR, OP. 98

Basic Texts for the Present Edition:

1. The score published by N. Simrock (publication number 8686).
2. Brahms's personal copy of the score, in the collection of the Gesellschaft der Musikfreunde, Vienna.

The symphony was completed in 1885 and published in 1886. Brahms's personal copy contains a few alterations that he entered in pencil; since these represent his final wishes, they have been taken into account in the present edition. The original versions of these passages, to be found in the Simrock edition of the full score and of the parts, are as follows:

In the 1st movement, 7th and 8th measures after the letter D, the 1st and 2nd violins originally had:

Likewise, in the recapitulation, 7th and 8th measures after N:

In the 3rd movement, the clarinet part in measures 14 through the 1st quarter note of 17 after the letter H was added later.

In other respects the Simrock edition is practically free of errors, apart from small technical inaccuracies.

The portrait in this volume is taken from a snapshot in the collection of Dr. Hellmuth von Hase on which Brahms appears together with Eugen d'Albert and Mr. and Mrs. Julius Klengel.

Hans Gál

Vienna
Spring, 1926

Symphony No. 1

in C Minor, Op. 68

324
a 2
Fl.
Ob.
Klar.
(B)
Fag.
K.-Fag.
(C)
Hr.
(Es)
Trpt.
(C)
Pk.
1.Viol.
2.Viol.
Br.
Vcl.
K.-B.
ff
f
sf
330

28

29

69
Fl.
Ob.
Klar. (A)
Fag.
Hr. (E)
1.Viol.
2.Viol.
Br.
Vcl.
K-B.
pizz.
arco
cresc.
76
D
dim.
dolce
espr.

61

J.B.1

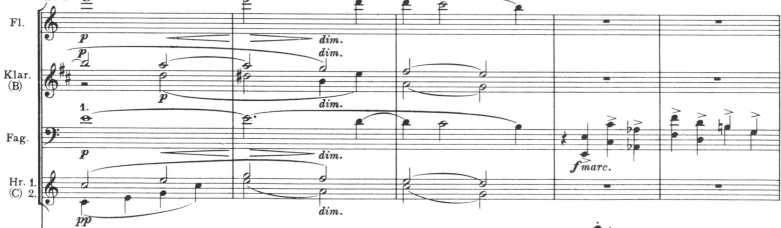

361
a 2
Q
Fl.
Ob.
Klar.
(B)
Fag.
K.-Fag.
(C)
Hr.
(Es)
Trpt.
(C)
Pos.
Pk.
1. Viol.
2. Viol.
Br.
Vcl.
K.-B.
fp
p
f
div.
pizz.
p marc.
Q

Più Allegro

Più Allegro

Symphony No. 2

in D Major, Op. 73

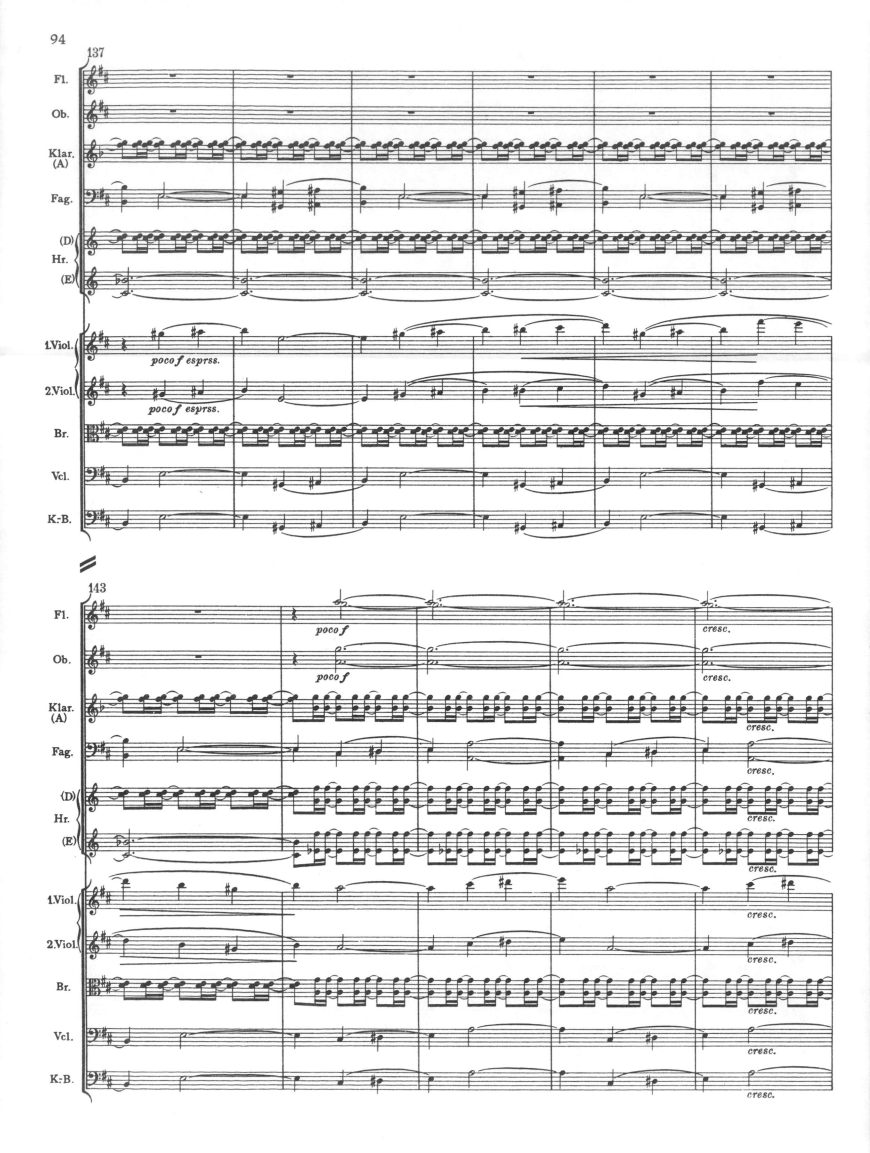

87
Fl.
Ob.
Klar. (A)
Fag.
Hr. (H)
Trpt. (H)
Pos. u. Btb.
Pk.
1. Viol.
2. Viol.
Br.
Vcl.
K.-B.
90
F
Fl.
Ob.
Klar. (A)
Fag.
Hr. (H)
Trpt. (H)
Pos.
Pk.
1. Viol.
2. Viol.
Br.
Vcl.
K.-B.
F

125

Presto ma non assai ($\mathtt{d} = \mathtt{d}$)

134

144

196
Fl.
Ob.
Klar. (A)
Fag.
(D) Hr. (E)
Trpt. (D)
Pos. u. Btb.
1.Viol.
2.Viol.
Br.
Vcl.
K.-B.
cresc.
marc.
ff
f
a 2
204
I Tranquillo
p
p dolce
I Tranquillo

148

395
a 2
Fl
Ob.
Klar.
(A)
Fag.
(D)
Hr.
(E)
Trpt.
(D)
Pos.
u.
Btb.
Pk.
1. Viol.
2. Viol.
Br.
Vcl.
u.K.-B.
404
a 2
Fl.
Ob.
Klar.
(A)
Fag.
(D)
Hr.
(E)
Trpt.
(D)
Pos.
u.
Btb.
Pk.
1. Viol.
2. Viol.
Br.
Vcl.
u.K.-B.

Symphony No. 3

in F Major, Op. 90

J. B. 3

231

218
Fl.
Ob.
Klar.
(B)
Fag.
K.-Fag.
(C)
Hr.
(F)
Trpt.
(F)
Pos.
Pk.
1.Viol.
2.Viol.
Br.
Vcl.
K.-B.
sff
sf
tr

Un poco sostenuto

Un poco sostenuto

Symphony No. 4

in E Minor, Op. 98

176
a 2
Fl.
Ob.
Klar. (A)
Fag.
Hr. (E) (C)
Trpt. (E)
1.Viol.
2.Viol.
Br.
Vcl.
K.-B.
ff
f
H
184
sotto voce
p
fpp
pp
Pk.

392
Q
a 2
Fl.
Ob.
Klar.
(A)
Fag.
(E)
Hr.
(C)
Trpt.
(E)
ff
1.Viol.
2.Viol.
Br.
Vcl.
K.-B.
400
sempre più f

281

A
15
Fl.
Ob.
Klar. (A)
Fag.
K.-Fag.
(E)
Hr.
(C)
Trpt. (E)
Pos.
Pk.
1.Viol.
2.Viol.
Br.
Vcl.
K.-B.
mp
cresc.
f ben marc.
p
a 2
ben marc.
mp ma marc.
div.
arco
f
A

325